Design and Build It to Play

Nikole Brooks Bethea

ROURKE'S
SCHOOL to HOME
CONNECTIONS
BEFORE AND DURING READING ACTIVITIES

Before Reading: *Building Background Knowledge and Vocabulary*

Building background knowledge can help children process new information and build upon what they already know. Before reading a book, it is important to tap into what children already know about the topic. This will help them develop their vocabulary and increase their reading comprehension.

Questions and Activities to Build Background Knowledge:

1. Look at the front cover of the book and read the title. What do you think this book will be about?
2. What do you already know about this topic?
3. Take a book walk and skim the pages. Look at the table of contents, photographs, captions, and bold words. Did these text features give you any information or predictions about what you will read in this book?

Vocabulary: *Vocabulary Is Key to Reading Comprehension*

Use the following directions to prompt a conversation about each word.

- Read the vocabulary words.
- What comes to mind when you see each word?
- What do you think each word means?

Vocabulary Words:

- *friction*
- *gravity*
- *momentum*
- *pulley*

During Reading: *Reading for Meaning and Understanding*

To achieve deep comprehension of a book, children are encouraged to use close reading strategies. During reading, it is important to have children stop and make connections. These connections result in deeper analysis and understanding of a book.

Close Reading a Text

During reading, have children stop and talk about the following:

- Any confusing parts
- Any unknown words
- Text to text, text to self, text to world connections
- The main idea in each chapter or heading

Encourage children to use context clues to determine the meaning of any unknown words. These strategies will help children learn to analyze the text more thoroughly as they read.

When you are finished reading this book, turn to the last page for an **After Reading Activity**.

Table of Contents

The Problem of Motion

How do you play? Do you ride bikes? Play sports? Go to amusement parks? When people play, they like to be in motion.

How do engineers design ways to help us move and play?

Zoom! Roller coaster cars run without engines. How do engineers make them go?

100

They put **gravity** to work! They put the tallest hill at the start of the ride. Gravity is the force that pulls the roller coaster cars down the hill. The taller the hill, the more gravity's pull works on the cars.

Momentum is the speed something gains once it is in motion.

The cars go faster as they zoom down the track. Their momentum carries them up the next hill. Momentum speeds the cars on and on to the end of the ride.

The Problem of Friction

Friction happens when moving things rub against each other. It slows things down.

How do engineers create less friction when a hook moves across a zip line?

Motion
Friction
Weight

They use a **pulley**. The pulley spins as it goes down the line. The spinning creates less friction.

The Problem of Safety

Playing can be dangerous. Bikers can fall off bikes. Baseball players can get hit with balls. Football players can be tackled. How do engineers keep us safe?

They design helmets to protect our heads. Imagine someone wearing a helmet gets hit in the head. The force of the hit goes into the helmet, not the person's head. The helmet spreads the force over a larger surface. The force on one spot is smaller.

Force on a helmet
Force spreading out
Force of the hit

Engineers also put padding inside helmets. When someone is hit, their head presses into the padding. This softens the force of the hit.

When engineers design to help us play, we stay safe and have a blast!

Photo Glossary

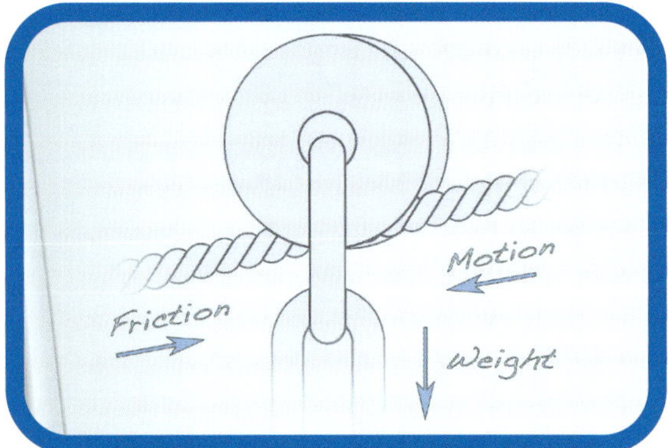

friction (FRIK-shuhn): The force that slows down objects when they rub against each other.

gravity (GRAV-i-tee): The force that pulls things toward the center of the Earth and keeps them from floating away.

momentum (moh-MEN-tuhm): The force or speed something gains when it is moving.

pulley (PUL-ee): A simple machine made of a wheel with a grooved rim on which a chain or rope can run.

Engineering Design Activity

What design will you use for a roller coaster?

Supplies

paper plates with a rim or lip around the outer edge
marble
scissors
clear tape
paper towel tubes, wooden building blocks, or other supports for the coaster
glue dots

Directions

Use paper plates to build a roller coaster that will carry a marble from the top to the bottom. Cut the rim off the plates. Join multiple plate rims together with tape. Create supports at different heights under the plates. Secure the plates to supports with glue dots. Does your marble make it from the top to the bottom?

Index

About the Author

In addition to writing children's science books, Nikole Brooks Bethea is a professional engineer. Her designs have included tall water tanks, systems to treat drinking water and wastewater, and underground water and wastewater utilities. She lives in the Florida Panhandle with her husband and four sons.

After Reading Activity

How do you like to play? Make a list of all the ways. Now, think about the engineering that went into creating the equipment and supplies used in your activities. Next to each item on the list, write what had to be designed or built so you could have fun.

Library of Congress PCN Data

Design and Build It to Play / Nikole Brooks Bethea
(My Engineering Library)
ISBN (hard cover)(alk. paper) 978-1-73163-852-6
ISBN (soft cover) 978-1-73163-929-5
ISBN (e-Book) 978-1-73164-006-2
ISBN (e-Pub) 978-1-73164-083-3
Library of Congress Control Number: 2020930263

Rourke Educational Media
Printed in the United States of America
01-1942011937

www.rourkeeducationalmedia.com

Edited by: Hailey Scragg
Cover and interior design by: Rhea Magaro-Wallace
Photo Credits: Cover logo: frog ©Eric Phol, test tube ©Sergey Lazarev, cover tab art ©siridhata, cover photo ©Andyd; page5: ©Cathy Yeulet; page 7: ©hanusst; pages 9, 22: ©VitalyEdush; pages 10, 11, 22: ©Tommy Alven; page 13: ©Yobro10; pages 14, 22: ©RossHelen; page 15: ©Roberto A Sanchez; page 17: (top left) ©CasarsaGuru, (top right) ©Wavebreakmedia, (bottom left) ©South_agency, (bottom right) ©Mark Tooker; pages 18, 19: ©skynesher, page 20: ©jpbcpa, page 21: ©kate_sept2004